TABLE OF CONTENTS

CRIME DOES NOT PAY

BUT IT SURE IS INTERESTING

Your stuff is sacred, and you want to keep your treasures safe! One of the best ways to do this is to keep it under lock and key—in an impenetrable vault, the strongest the world has ever known!

You can build one with the security vault activity kit included with this book. You'll find instructions at the back on pages 26–31.

It also helps to understand the minds of slick and daring criminals—some who have succeeded in pulling off the world's splashiest, most costly **heists**, and others who have tried and failed. The crooks you'll learn about in this book got away with stealing millions—and in one case, a billion bucks—until they got caught.

IN THIS BOOK YOU WILL READ CASE FILES OF UNSCRUPULOUS BANDITS, SUCH AS:

BANK BURGLARS

JEWEL THIEVES

ART THIEVES

Read their stories. Find out what makes big-time crooks tick. See how they got caught.

AS THICK AS THIEVES

Robbing anyone of anything is a criminal act and is no laughing matter! When they are caught, these criminals do hard time behind bars. They may think their schemes are worth it at the time, but in the end, they are not.

Now, turn the page for a word of caution from our sponsors.

5 GREAT HEIST MOVIES

5. THE GREAT MUPPET CAPER

4. ANT-MAN

3. THE NUT JOB

2. SLY COOPER

1. THE PINK PANTHER

People spend a lot of time online these days, because of that, **cyber theft** is becoming more common than **robberies** committed in real life. But there are ways you can stay safe when you're online.

1. Never give any private information—such as your name, address, phone number, or passwords—to someone you don't know.

2. Don't shop with credit cards if you're in a spot without private, protected Internet service. (Hint: Home may be okay, but a coffee shop's Wi-Fi likely is not.)

3. Think before you click! If you receive an email with an attachment from someone you don't know, don't open it. Delete it or show it to an adult. Clicking can start a virus that will share your files with someone else. And to get them back, you may be asked to pay a lot of money. This ransomware is a modern-day heist!

And now we return you to your regularly scheduled programming, already in progress.

GEAR AND TACTICS

Guns and explosives are one route to robbing, but the most competent and successful thieves have more interesting tricks up their sleeves.

TUNNELING TOOLS

These might include explosives and a **thermal lance** that cuts through steel.

PAINT

A group of glamorous, highly successful Serbian thieves seemed to have thought of everything. In a heist in France, they undertook the simple act of painting a park bench across from where they would be operating and left a "Wet Paint" sign. That way, no one was hanging around to watch the break-in.

VACUUM CLEANER

Rather than breaking into a vault, a group in France successfully robbed a number of stores by breaking into the **pneumatic tube** through which cash flows, and sucking it all out with a fancied-up vacuum.

PERFECT TIMING

This is probably the most useful tool a team of **burglars** has. You'll read that a lot of heists take place over three-day weekends. This extra day gives a team just enough time to get a big job done without attracting notice.

...STED! Even with the
...rs aligning perfectly,
...ice solve over 65 percent
...armed robberies.

Let the countdown begin through the ten heftiest heists of all time!

THE *SWEDISH*
HELICOPTER HEIST

Swedish police noticed that a robbery-by-helicopter was being planned. They had been conducting **surveillance**. Unfortunately, they had been conducting surveillance in the wrong city!

$5 MILLION

A stolen helicopter landed on the roof of a cash depot in Sweden. Three bandits dressed entirely in black leaped out. Working fast, they axed their way through the roof and lowered themselves in. They torched through security doors, packed up millions, and lugged the loot back up into the stolen chopper. Some police arrived, but it wasn't the right unit, so they were powerless to act. The thugs escaped in the chopper in full sight of the coppers.

CRIME ANALYSIS

MISSION
Steal a helicopter, drive it to a cash depot, blast in, take enormous amounts of cash and fly off

TARGET
A large, well-stocked cash depot in Västberga, Sweden

SECURITY
Alarms, security doors, and police

THE GETAWAY
A stolen Bell 206 Jet Ranger helicopter, later found ditched

MASTERMIND[S]

A Serbian crime group, including former members of an elite special forces police unit

HOW DID THEY DO IT?

With helicopter, a sledgehammer, a rope, and nerves of steel!

After the largest cash robbery in Swedish history, officials worried that cash would be unavailable to banks and stores.

DID THEY GET CAUGHT?

Not that day! They had outfoxed the Swedish helicopter police with a bomb scare at their own helicopter pad. But yes, the thieves were eventually caught and all sentenced to jail. Hardly any loot was recovered.

RAID OF THE
SOCIÉTÉ GÉNÉRALE BANK
$10 MILLION

A photographer in the South of France realized that the local bank vault can be accessed through the floor if he tunneled through a... sewer? Would it be worth it? For a cool, smelly $10 million, he thinks, *"Mais, oui!"* (That's "heck, yeah" in French.)

ALBERT SPAGG

Spaggiari never did time, and would sometimes tease French police by having his picture published in the paper, with a caption reading "Hello from Albert."

CRIME ANALYSIS

MISSION
Tunnel through a sewer toward a huge quantity of cash and jewels

TARGET
The Société Générale Bank in Nice, France

SECURITY
Super-thick walls and a door with two locks that needed to be turned at the exact same time! There was no way anyone was getting in. Oh, unless they drilled through the floor—once in, the vault wasn't even armed!

THE GETAWAY
The tunnel, of course

MASTERMIND[S]
Albert Spaggiari was the mastermind. He went on and on, bragging about the crime, but he wouldn't give up his gang.

HOW DID THEY DO IT?
A crew of twenty tunneled in over a holiday weekend. They brought wine and food, and stayed a full three days before moving all the loot. Weird vacation!

DID THEY GET CAUGHT?
Spaggiari did, but then he escaped! He leaped out of a judge's window and jumped onto the back of a motorcycle that was waiting for him. He was never seen again.

BREAK-IN AT
BANCO CENTRAL

$72 MILLION

Renting office space in a building two blocks away from Banco Central in Brazil, this landscaping company was just a front Luis Fernando Ribeiro and his
to tunnel down, over, and across the street to gain undisturbed, inside access to the bank's $72 million in cash!

CRIME ANALYSIS

MISSION
Tunnel into Central Bank of Brazil without attracting attention

TARGET
The Central Bank of Brazil, which controls the country's money supply

SECURITY
Internal alarms and sensors

THE GETAWAY
They left the way they came!

MASTERMIND[S]
Luis Fernando Ribiero and 25 accomplices

HOW DID THEY DO IT?
They dug 13 ft. (3.96 m) down, made a tunnel more than 250 ft. (76.2 m) long with its own lighting and venting system, and blasted through nearly 4 ft. (1.22 m) of steel-reinforced concrete to enter the bank vault.

DID THEY GET CAUGHT?
Eight have been arrested; the rest have not. Ribeiro was kidnapped before he was arrested. And after his **ransom** was paid, his kidnappers killed him anyway. Only about an eighth of the money was recovered.

The money weighed more than 3 tons. That's 6,000 lbs. (2721.55 kg)!

UNITED CALIFORNIA
BANK BURGLARY

$30 MILLION

On March 24, 1972, master thief Amil Dinisio and his team broke into the safe deposit vault of United California Bank. At $30 million in cash and valuables, which is $100 million by today's standards, this was the biggest heist in history at the time. It was the perfect crime. Well, almost perfect.

CRIME ANALYSIS

MISSION
To enter an extremely well-protected vault through its weakest point: the roof

TARGET
The United California Bank

SECURITY
One outer alarm, one inner alarm, and a vault with an incredibly thick door

THE GETAWAY
A 1962 Oldsmobile Super 88—the perfect ride for a '70s heist

MASTERMIND[S]
Amil Dinsio along with his brother, nephews, and brothers-in-law

HOW DID THEY DO IT?
They disabled the bank's alarm by filling it with liquid Styrofoam. They drilled a hole in the roof to disable another alarm. Dynamite destroyed the roof and bags of dirt made it collapse in rather than explode outward. They used a custom sledgehammer to open safety deposit boxes. They robbed over the course of Friday, Saturday, and Sunday nights.

DID THEY GET CAUGHT?

The gang left dirty dishes in their hideout. DNA evidence from the fingerprinted, dirty plates jailed Dinsio for 10 years. His accomplices got 3 to 5 years, and only some of the money was recovered.

GRAND THEFT AT THE ANTWERP WORLD DIAMOND CENTER

An illustration of the vault at the Antwerp World Diamond Center

$100 MILLION

In the diamond capital of the world, sat a vault with ten layers of security and constant surveillance. How could a small-time jewel merchant work around every obstacle to pull off a heist this huge at a place this well protected?

CRIME ANALYSIS

MISSION
Disable one of the world's greatest security systems to access one of the world's greatest treasures

TARGET
The two vault floors beneath the Antwerp World Diamond Center

THE GETAWAY
Notarbartolo drove the loot home. Others walked back to his apartment.

MASTERMIND[S]
Leonardo Notabartolo and his accomplices "the Monster," "the Wizard of Keys," "the Genius," and "Speedy"

HOW DID THEY DO IT?
Notabartolo claimed he and his team overcame every antitheft obstacle, but their story is so complex that others suspect the break-in was an inside job.

DID THEY GET CAUGHT?
Yep. A salami sandwich wrapper left in the woods along with a few diamonds had DNA evidence, linking Notarbartolo to 1) salami in his apartment, 2) a receipt for salami found in his apartment, and 3) a video of "the Monster" buying the very same salami.

HISTORY OF THE
HARRY WINSTON HEISTS

$108 MILLION

Just before Christmas 2008, four women—actually, men wearing flowing wigs, dresses, and dark glasses—were buzzed into a swanky, well-protected jewel boutique in Paris. They gathered more than $80 million worth of precious gems. But the real surprise was that one year earlier, they pulled off a similar heist, that time dressed as a painting crew!

CRIME ANALYSIS

MISSION
To ransack a jewel boutique frequented by the rich and famous—for the second time!

TARGET
Piles of rubies, emeralds, and diamonds

SECURITY
A locked door with an intercom system—and a crooked security guard!

THE GETAWAY
The rogues made what was probably an unladylike getaway into a waiting car.

MASTERMIND[S]
A Frenchman named Douadi "Doudou" Yahiaoui and seven accomplices

It was at first believed that an elite Eastern European group of jewel thieves and former soldiers were to blame. Instead, it was some thugs who lived in the suburbs of Paris.

HOW DID THEY DO IT?
They relied on disguises and surprise to get in.

DID THEY GET CAUGHT?
Eight men including the security guard were caught. But it took seven years to get them behind bars! Nineteen million dollars of the loot was found stuffed into a drainpipe outside Paris.

THE SCHIPHOL AIRPORT
ATTACK

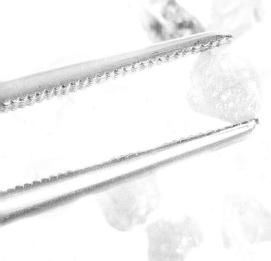

$118 MILLION

Jewels don't travel first class, silly! They're flown in freight planes. One such plane at Amsterdam's main airport stood ready to be loaded with $118 million worth of diamonds, when two guys dressed in airline uniforms and driving an airline truck ambushed an **armored truck** full of diamonds on its way to deliver them to the plane. The diamonds missed their flight, and the thieves were never caught.

CRIME ANALYSIS

MISSION
To intercept diamonds en route to Antwerp

TARGET
A truck carrying $118 million worth of precious cargo

SECURITY
State-of-the-art airport security and an armored truck

THE GETAWAY
The thieves drove off of the airport premises in the airline truck, which was later found burned out in the woods near a town called Hoofddorp.

MASTERMIND[S]
If only we knew!

HOW DID THEY DO IT?
The details are sketchy, but it is believed that the thieves gained access to the freight portion of the airport, slipped past security, and got out of there fast.

DID THEY GET CAUGHT?
Not yet! And the loot has not been recovered.

THE CITY BONDS
MUGGING

$460 MILLION

On a lovely spring day in London, John Goddard was doing his job as a messenger for a financial company—walking down the street with a suitcase containing 301 **bearer bonds** valued at $1 million apiece—until a thug pulls a knife on him. Goddard gave up the briefcase, making one of the largest heists in history seem like a walk in the park!

Banks were warned not to cash the stolen bonds. Some time later, someone was caught trying to cash the bonds in the United States. That person gave up prime suspect, Keith Cheeseman, who was then sentenced.

CRIME ANALYSIS

MISSION
Steal and cash in hundreds of bearer bonds. Worth about $1 million apiece, these bonds were as good as cash for whoever has them.

TARGET
A financial company called Sheppards, a London brokerage. John Goddard was its messenger.

SECURITY
NONE! None at all!

THE GETAWAY
No special getaway vehicle was needed. The thieves just ran off with the bonds.

MASTERMIND[S]
One was a small-time crook and the other a well-known fraudster. They might have had organized crime connections in the United States.

HOW DID THEY DO IT?
The gang obviously knew the route the messenger would take. Pulling one knife on him did it.

DID THEY GET CAUGHT?
One suspect, likely the mugger, was found shot dead before he could be arrested. Career criminal Keith Cheeseman was caught, jumped bail, and fled England. Later, he was sentenced to 6½ years in prison. None of the money was recovered.

THE MYSTERIOUS
ISABELLA STEWART
GARDNER MUSEUM

The frames where the precious paintings hung remain empty as a reminder of the one of the grandest art thefts in history. They're also ready for the artwork to be replaced in them when it is recovered.

$500 MILLION

Sometime after midnight on St. Patrick's Day 1990, two guys costumed as Boston cops—one wearing a fake mustache—knocked and asked to be let into the Isabella Stewart Gardner Museum so they could "check a disturbance in the garden." When the museum guards let them in, the crooks tied them up and left with $500 million worth of art. Gulp!

CRIME ANALYSIS

MISSION   To pull off one of the largest art robberies in history

TARGET   The Isabella Stewart Gardner Museum in Boston

SECURITY   In addition to locked doors and (ineffective) guards, the museum was outfitted with motion detectors and video cameras.

MASTERMIND[S]   If only we knew!

THE GETAWAY

A car with $500 million of art crammed into it

HOW DID THEY DO IT?

Some people suspect it was an inside job–that one of the guards was involved, but that's been too hard to prove. Maybe the guards were just surprised. Whatever the case, the two thieves sliced precious paintings out of their frames and disappeared.

The museum has offered a $5 million reward—as well as instructions of how to care for paintings properly in the meantime: they should be kept away from light and at around 70° Fahrenheit and be kept wrapped in acid-free paper.

DID THEY GET CAUGHT?

No! In 2013 the FBI announced that they thought they knew their identities. Now they say they think the two suspects are dead.

CRIME AT THE CENTRAL
BANK OF IRAQ

In 2014 a group called ISIS attacked another branch of the Central Bank in Iraq—also taking hundreds of millions of dollars.

$1 BILLION

As the United States and Iraq maneuvered toward war in 2003, President George W. Bush ordered dictator Saddam Hussein out of his own country. Before he went into hiding, Hussein sent one of his sons to the bank with a note demanding $1 billion in American cash. This is far beyond what he had available in his own account. But no one says no to a dictator, so bank employees packed up and loaded $100 bills into multiple tractor-trailers!

CRIME ANALYSIS

MISSION
Take $1 billion from the local bank, maybe to pay for war efforts or maybe to get more palaces? (He had already built more than 20.)

TARGET
The Central Bank of Iraq

SECURITY
Security goes by the wayside when a dictator starts making demands!

THE GETAWAY
Tractor-trailer trucks!

MASTERMIND[S]
Saddam, his son Qusay, and his personal assistant Abid al-Hamid Mahmood

HOW DID THEY DO IT?

Saddam wrote a note to the bank demanding $1 billion, and he got it. "When you get an order from Saddam Hussein, you do not discuss it," said an Iraqi official, who also worked at the bank.

The day after Saddam Hussein took the money, the United States bombed Iraq.

DID THEY GET CAUGHT?

No. Though, in unrelated events, Qusay died in battle, and Hussein was executed.

LOCK IT UP!

BUILD YOUR OWN SECURITY VAULT

Now that you know how these savvy stickup artists think, it's your turn to outsmart them. Follow the instructions on the next few pages to customize your own state-of-the-art quadruple-security vault to protect your vulnerable valuables.

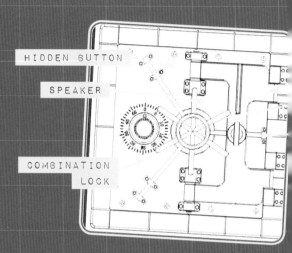

HIDDEN BUTTON

SPEAKER

COMBINATION LOCK

COMPONENTS

(A) Side Panel Key x4

(B) Password Lock Bar

(C) Key Card

(D) Key

(E) Back Panel

(F) Front Panel

DC1.5V X 2
SIZE AAA/LR03
Requires two AAA batteries

(G) Battery Cover

MAKE SURE YOU HAVE ALL THE
COMPONENTS BEFORE YOU BEGIN

Connect the four side panels (A) as shown below.

KEY CARD SLOT

FAKE LOCK

KEYHOLE

Attach the back panel (E) to the assembled side panels as shown below.

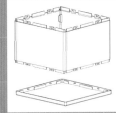

Attach the front panel (F) to the assembled side panels as shown below.

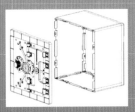

Insert the key card (C) all the way across the key card slot. Insert the key (D) into the keyhole, and turn the key (D) to the right until it is in a horizontal position. Open the front panel (F) door by pulling the combination lock. If you cannot open the door, rotate the combination lock to the right and stop at 5, then rotate to the left and stop at 12. You should now be able to open the door by pulling the combination lock.

Unscrew the battery cover (G) on the back of the front panel (F), and insert two new AAA batteries into the battery compartment. Make sure the batteries are placed in the proper (+) (-) position as indicated inside the battery compartment. Use a screwdriver to secure the battery cover (G) to the back of the front panel (F).

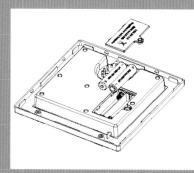 

 Close the front panel (F) door. You will hear a "door close" sound, which indicates the device has been activated. If you do not hear a "door close" sound, make sure the batteries are working and correctly installed.

 Rotate the combination lock to a random number.

 Turn the key (D) to the left until it is in a vertical position and then remove the key (C) from the keyhole.

 Remove the key card (C) from the key card slot.

 Assembly is now complete. After thirty seconds, you will hear three beeps, which indicate the alarm of the quadruple-security vault is now activated.

CONGRATULATIONS! YOUR QUADRUPLE-SECURITY VAULT IS NOW READY TO USE!

How to Open the Quadruple-Security Vault and Deactivate the Alarm

 Press the hidden button. You will hear a "hidden button" sound followed by three beeps. These three beeps indicate you can proceed.
Note: If you proceed to step 2 without hearing the three beeps in step 1, the alarm will sound when you open the door.

 Insert the key card (C) into the key card slot. You will hear a "key card" sound followed by three beeps, which indicate you can proceed.
Note: If you take out the key card (C) after step 2, the alarm will sound when you open the door.

 Insert the key (D) into the keyhole, and turn the key (D) to the right until it is in a horizontal position.

 Rotate the combination lock to the right and stop at 5, then rotate to the left and stop at 12. The door will open and you will hear an "open door" sound.
Note: If you pause during the steps for more than one minute or do not open the quadruple-security vault for one minute after you complete step 4, you will hear three beeps, which indicate the quadruple-security vault alarm has been reactivated. To open the quadruple-security vault without setting off the alarm, you will have to repeat steps 1 to 4.

How to Close the Quadruple-Security Vault and Activate the Alarm

 Close the quadruple-security vault door. You will hear a "close door" sound.
Note: Make sure that the flat edges of the inside parts of the lock are aligned with the door or the door will not shut all the way.

 Rotate the combination lock to a random number to lock the quadruple-security vault door.

Turn the key (D) to the left until it is in a vertical position and then remove the key (D) from the keyhole.

 Remove the key card (C) from the key card slot.

 After thirty seconds, you will hear three beeps, which indicate the alarm of the quadruple-security vault has been activated.
Note: If you do not remove the key card (C) from the quadruple-security vault, the quadruple-security vault alarm will not turn on.

How to Disarm the Alarm

 Make sure the key card (C) and the key (D) are not inserted into the quadruple-security vault.

 Press the hidden button. You will hear a "hidden button" sound.

 Insert the key card (C) into the key card slot. You will hear a "key card" sound, and the alarm will stop.

 Remove the key card (C) from the device to activate the alarm again.
Note: If you forget to remove the key card (C) from the device, the alarm will activate automatically after one minute.

Alert: If someone activates the alarm and does not stop the alarm correctly, the alarm will sound for thirty seconds. The next time you try to open the quadruple-security vault by pressing the hidden button, you will hear five beeps before the "hidden button" sound to indicate someone tried to open the quadruple-security vault.

Default combination lock password: Rotate the combination dial to the right and stop at 5, then rotate left and stop at 12.

You can use the default combination lock password or you can select any of the three preset passwords. To select any of the three preset passwords, please follow these steps:

1. Open the quadruple-security vault door by following the directions in the "How to Open the Quadruple-Security Vault and Deactivate the Alarm" section.

2. On the back of the combination dial, you will see the numbers 1 through 4, which identify the four different password options.
   • Password #1 (default combination lock password) – Rotate right and stop at 5, then rotate left and stop at number 12.
   • Password #2 – Rotate right and stop at 43, then rotate left and stop at 12.
   • Password #3 – Rotate right and stop at 30, then rotate left and stop at 12.
   • Password #4 – Rotate right and stop at 17, then rotate left and stop at 12.

3. To change the combination, rotate and remove the password lock bar (B) as shown below.

PASSWORD LOCK

PASSWORD LOCK HOLE

PASSWORD LOCK BAR

4. Insert the password lock bar (B) into the hole of your new selected password number. You will find an engraved number next to the hole that indicates the password number.

5. Move the password lock bar (B) back in the password lock as shown below to secure your new password selection.

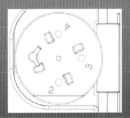

6. Close the security vault door.

GLOSSARY

ACCOMPLICES:

people who help someone do something that is wrong

ARMORED TRUCK:

a secure truck with strong locks, doors, and usually bulletproof glass that transports money and valuables to or from banks or other businesses

BEARER BONDS:

coupon-like documents that have an assigned monetary value and are owned by whomever possesses them

BURGLARS:

people who break into buildings to steal something

CYBER THEFT:

the use of Internet-connected computers to steal an identity, personal information, or financial information to use illegally

HEISTS:

robberies or—for the purposes of this book—thefts on a grand scale

PNEUMATIC TUBE:

a tube that transports cylinder-like containers using compressed air, like the drive-thru tubes at your parent's bank

RANSOM:

money paid to free someone who's been kidnapped

ROBBERY:

using violence or fear to steal someone's property

SURVEILLANCE:

closely watching someone or something in order to prevent a crime

THERMAL LANCE:

a tool that heats and cuts through steel and is also known as a burning bar